STORAGE

IN THE SAME SERIES

Oil Processing
Fruit and Vegetable Processing
Root Crop Processing
Fish Processing
Cereal Processing
Drying
Women's Roles in Technical Innovation

Food Cycle Technology Source Books

STORAGE

Practical Action Publishing Ltd
27a Albert Street, Rugby, CV21 2SG, Warwickshire, UK
www.practicalactionpublishing.org

First published by Practical Action Publishing in 1995

Transferred to digital printing in 2008

ISBN 10: 1 85339 309 6
ISBN 13: 978 1 85339 309 9
ISBN Library Ebook: 9781780444321
Book DOI: http://dx.doi.org/10.3362/9781780444321

Since 1974, Practical Action Publishing has published and disseminated books and
information in support of international development work throughout the world.
Practical Action Publishing is a trading name of Practical Action Publishing Ltd
(Company Reg. No. 1159018), the wholly owned publishing company of Practical
Action. Practical Action Publishing trades only in support of its parent charity objectives
and any profits are covenanted back to Practical Action (Charity Reg. No. 247257, Group
VAT Registration No. 880 9924 76).

Illustrations by Matthew Whitton
Typeset by Dorwyn Ltd, Rowlands Castle, Hants, UK

Preface

This source book is one of a continuing UNIFEM series which aims to increase awareness of the range of technological options and sources of expertise, as well as indicating the complex nature of designing and successfully implementing technology development and dissemination programmes.

UNIFEM was established in 1976, and is an autonomous body associated since 1984 with the United Nations Development Programme. UNIFEM seeks to free women from under-productive tasks and augment the productivity of their work as a means of accelerating the development process. It does this through funding specific women's projects which yield direct benefits and through actions directed to ensure that all development policies, plans, programmes and projects take account of the needs of women producers.

In recognition of women's special roles in the production, processing, storage, preparation and marketing of food, UNIFEM initiated a Food Cycle Technology project in 1985 with the aim of promoting the widespread diffusion of tested technologies to increase the productivity of women's labour in this sector. While global in perspective, the initial phase of the project was implemented in Africa in view of the concern over food security in many countries of the region.

A careful evaluation of the Africa experience in the final phase of this five-year programme showed that there was a need for catalytic interventions which would lead to an enabling environment for women to have easier access to technologies. This would be an environment where women producers could obtain information on the available technologies, have the capacity to analyse such information, make technological choices on their own, and acquire credit and training to enable the purchase and operation of the technology of their choice. This UNIFEM source book series aims to facilitate the building of such an environment.

Acknowledgements

This series of food cycle technology source books has been prepared at Intermediate Technology (IT) in the United Kingdom within the context of UNIFEM's Women and Food Cycle Technologies specialization. Translation and printing of the books is undertaken by the Italian Association for Women in Development (AIDOS).

During the preparation process, the project staff contacted numerous project directors, rural development agencies, technology centres, women's organizations, equipment manufacturers and researchers in all parts of the world.

The authors wish to thank the many agencies and individuals who have contributed to the preparation of this source book. Special thanks are owed to Clare Sheffield for preparation of the manuscript, Ian Macwhinnie for editing and Matthew Whitton for the illustrations. In addition to those listed in the contacts section, the authors would also like to thank John New, Emma Crewe, Kithsiri Dharmapriya, Barrie Axtell, Paul Douglas, Simon Burne, Bertha Msora, Abdullah Al-Mahmud and Jim McDowell.

The preparation of the first five source books has been funded by UNIFEM with a cost-sharing contribution from the Government of Italy and the Government of the Netherlands. The Government of Italy provided the funds for continuation of the series, as well as the translation and printing of the source books.

Peggy Oti-Boateng
UNIFEM Consultant
University of Science and Technology, Kumasi, Ghana

Mike Battcock
IT Consultant, Rugby, UK

Contents

INTRODUCTION ix

1 The importance of storage 1

2 Principles of storage 2

Temperature 2
Moisture 3
Keeping pests out of the store 3
Control of pests in stores 5
Storage characteristics of selected food commodities 6

3 Traditional storage methods 9

Earthenware pots and gourds 9
Leaves 10
Bark 10
Baskets 11
Sacks 12
Basket silos 13
Roof storage 14
Maize cribs 15
Underground pits 16
Clamp storage 16
Small storehouses 17
Earth silos 18

4 Improved storage techniques 19

Plastic bags 19
45-gallon metal drums 20
The Pusa bin 20
Metal silos 21
Brick and ferro-cement silos 22
Storage in ventilated huts 23
Improved pit storage 24

5 Socio-economic context 25

Appraisal 25
Technology choice 26
Economic considerations 27
Social and cultural considerations 28
Monitoring and evaluation 29

6 Case studies   30

   Improvements to traditional grain stores in Zambia   30
   Flexible solar heat disinfestation devices for domestic and rural storage
   of cereals in the tropics   31

REFERENCES   32

CONTACTS   34

Introduction

THE MAJORITY of the population of the developing world is occupied in one way or another with the production of food. Without proper regulation of agricultural production, linked to food preservation, processing and storage policies, any increase in agricultural production can lead to harvest peaks with correspondingly low prices. The use of appropriate storage technologies is an important way of improving food security and lowering the risk of famine in the months preceding the harvest.

Storage is an integral part of the food processing chain. While this source book concentrates on the storage of basic commodities such as grains and root crops, major foods such as oils, fish and fresh produce are also covered. The storage of finished goods, which have been processed, is outside the scope of this source book and is covered in other books in the series.

After briefly considering the importance of storage, this source book examines the basic principles involved in storage and looks at traditional storage methods and improved techniques. The book ends with selected case studies. These proved extremely difficult to locate. It is not clear whether this is because very few women are involved in storage projects, or simply due to lack of documentation.

A list of specialized institutions able to advise on storage matters can be found in the Appendix.

1
The importance of storage

GOOD STORAGE FACILITIES are important to farmers all over the world. They help to ensure household and community food security until the next harvest, and commodities for sale can be held back so that farmers can avoid being forced to sell at low prices in the glut that often follows a harvest. While considerable losses can occur in the field, both before and during harvest, the greatest losses usually occur during storage.

The basic objective of good storage is to create environmental conditions which protect the product and maintain its quality and its quantity, thus reducing product loss and financial loss.

Loss in quantity

Loss shows up as a loss of weight of the foodstuff due to it being eaten by insects, rodents and birds or to drying of the product. These weight losses are not always visually apparent. For example, some insects will eat only the centres of grain kernels so, even though the volume of grain may appear to remain the same, there can be considerable weight loss.

Quality-related losses

Losses of this type can be nutritional, or chemical. They may be caused by contamination with toxic moulds or foreign matter. Pests that selectively eat a part of the foodstuff (such as the nutritious germ of the grain) will reduce the value of the foodstuff as a whole. Other causes of loss include the loss of vitamins through the action of sunlight and temperature.

Chemical changes are particularly common in fatty foods through the development of rancidity. Some moulds, particularly *Aspergillus flavus*, produce toxins, one of the most common being aflatoxin. Aflatoxin-producing moulds can grow on many products, but maize, coconuts and peanuts are particularly susceptible. These toxins pose a long-term health risk.

General contamination can occur in many ways and shows up in such forms as insect fragments, rodent hairs, excreta and urine, as well as dust and other materials that enter the product vicinity through human mishandling. The presence of rat urine can cause serious problems as rats are carriers of Weil's Disease. Sieving is often used to reduce the obvious signs of foreign matter contamination.

There are two reasons for food storage: domestic security and maintaining value prior to sale. Farmers may not accept improvements which incur costs when storing primarily for home consumption. There are many reasons for this. For instance, an improvement in the quality of a food produced for home consumption is not reflected in a higher monetary value.

Farmers may well be open to making improvements to storage systems when they can see a potential financial advantage. It should be borne in mind that farmers have, over a long period, developed traditional stores that can work well. In many cases, these need only small improvements to make the difference between simply having enough for subsistence and creating a surplus for sale.

2
Principles of storage

MOST DEVELOPING COUNTRIES are in the tropics, often in areas of high rainfall and humidity. These conditions are ideal for the development of micro-organisms and insects which cause high levels of deterioration of crops in store. Food losses during storage are the result of the biological, chemical or physical damage briefly described in the previous chapter.

In order to reduce the amount of food lost, the environment in the store needs to be controlled so as to lower the possibility of:

* biological damage by insects, rodents and micro-organisms;
* chemical damage through rancidity development and flavour changes, etc.;
* physical damage through crushing, breaking, etc.

Good storage thus involves controlling the following factors:

* temperature
* moisture
* light
* pests
* hygiene

Temperature

The temperature within a store is affected by the sun, the cooling effect of radiation from the store, outside air temperatures, heat generated by the respiration of both the food in store and any insects present.

With a few exceptions, micro-organisms thrive in environments with temperatures between 10 and 60°C. Insects have a narrower range which generally lies between 16 and 45°C. As stores in most parts of the tropics and sub-tropics have temperatures between 25 and 35°C, the effects of both micro-organisms and insects are obviously very important. Direct temperature control of small stores is not usually a technical or economic possibility so other measures, particularly reducing the moisture content of the stored produce, are necessary.

One simple measure of insect control involving heat is commonly used. This is generally known as sunning and involves the product, such as grain, being laid out in a thin layer in the hot sunlight. The insects tend to leave the grain if the temperature reaches 40–45°C. It should be noted that sunning does not always destroy eggs or larvae.

Incorrect store temperatures can result in biological and chemical damage to the foodstuff being stored. Examples include the loss of germination ability in seed materials and the accumulation of sugars in commodities such as potato and sweet potato which need relatively low storage temperatures.

Temperature also affects chemical damage. The speed of chemical change in a food depends upon the temperature and the food's moisture content. A 10°C rise in temperature causes an approximately two-fold increase in the rate of reaction. Thus, cold storage will retard such changes as fat oxidation and vitamin loss. Many dried foods benefit from even a small reduction in their storage temperature, and cool and dry conditions can greatly reduce the rate of development of brown discoloration and off-flavours.

Incorrect temperature control can result in physical damage. At high temperatures, fats in products may melt, while at low temperatures, sugar in sweet foods may crystallize.

It should be noted that for root crops, as well as fruits and other vegetables, temperatures should not be too low, otherwise chilling injury will occur due to the plant cells rupturing. Yams and cassava, being of tropical origin, do not require storage temperatures as low as potatoes and sweet potatoes. Considerable tissue disruption may occur when foods are frozen. The worst effects are seen in foods slowly cooled to below their freezing point. Freezing also destroys the stability of emulsions, and foods such as milk and cheese may show a marked separation of fat upon thawing.

Moisture

All micro-organisms, including moulds, require moisture to survive and multiply. If the moisture content in a product going into store is low enough, micro-organisms will be unable to grow, provided that the moisture in the store is also kept low. Moisture should therefore be prevented from entering the store.

All materials that have been dried will try to come back into equilibrium with the climate around them and in tropical countries this usually means absorbing moisture. The moisture level below which micro-organisms cannot grow is referred to as the safe moisture content. The table below lists the safe moisture content levels for cereals and pulses, valid for temperatures up to 27°C. Slight variations in safe moisture contents arise, depending upon the variety.

While in general it is essential that all foodstuffs are below their safe moisture content before they enter the store, the safe moisture content is to some extent related to the required storage time. Moisture levels above the safe moisture

Table 1. Safe moisture content levels for cereals and pulses stored below 27°C

Product		Safe moisture content (%)
Cereals:	maize flour	11.5
	maize (shelled)	13.5
	millet	16.0
	rice (milled)	13.0
	rice	15.0
	sorghum	13.5
	wheat	13.5
	wheat flour	12.0
Pulses:	broad bean, cow pea	15.0
	lentil, pea	14.0

content can be tolerated if only short storage times are required.

The siting and the ventilation of the store are important. Condensation of moisture can cause storage problems. If the walls of a store are cooled below their dew point by low night temperatures, condensation can occur and increase the moisture in the layers of produce near the edge of the store.

It is important to remember that most stored food products are 'alive' and respiring, giving off moisture as well as heat.

Moisture can also cause physical changes. Products such as cane sugar, salt and milk powder will absorb moisture from the atmosphere and 'cake'. Absorption of moisture by dried fruits may lead to sugar crystallization.

Keeping pests out of the store

Mammals

The most serious pests for store owners are rodents. A wide range of measures are available which mainly depend on denying hem access to the store. All holes and entrances to the store should be fitted with fine wire mesh. The building should, if possible, be on poles with rat baffles around them as shown in the diagram. If the building is situated under a tree, rats can readily gain access on to the roof. The ground around the store should be cleared and all sources of water denied to rodents. They can easily gnaw through wooden doors so tin plate should be fixed to the bottom 30cm of the door.

Domestic animals such as goats and poultry can pose a problem and should be kept at a distance from the store by building simple protective fences.

Insects

The main purpose of insect control is to prevent insects entering the storage containers. The containers should be closed tightly; baskets may be smeared with mud to seal them. Acces to the store by insects such as ants and termites can be prevented by building the store on poles which are treated with coal tar, green camphor oil, or covered with fat or waste oil. Surrounding the supporting poles with a layer of sieved wood ashes, and sinking the poles into ground soaked with waste oil, will also deter insects.

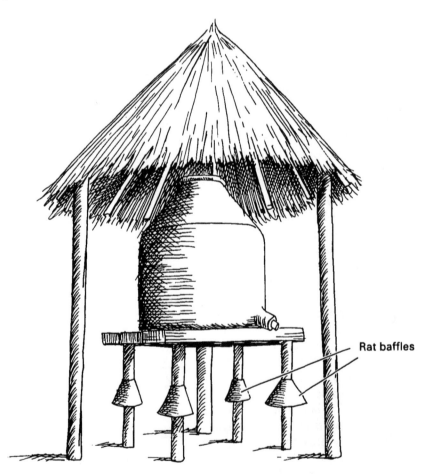

Rat baffles

Food store showing rat baffles

The smoke and heat of a fire will kill or drive insects away from stored produce. For this reason, many traditional household stores are built in the roof of the house or over the cooking fire.

Mixing the produce with materials such as wood ash, burnt cow dung, fine sand, lime and certain clays deters insects, mainly by scratching their bodies, which causes them to lose water and die. The use of such commonly available additives is an alternative to synthetic insecticides especially for the protection of seed material. Certain vegetable oils such as palm oil and groundnut oil can be applied to pulses to give protection against bruchids (beetles).

In many parts of the world the roots, leaves, fruits and flowers of local plants are known to act as an insect repellent. Notable examples are neem leaves, derris and pyrethrum.

It is common practice to store cereals unthreshed in order to give some protection against insects. Husks, pods and outer coverings offer some protection against insect attack provided they are undamaged. Traditional maize varieties often have a husk which covers the whole cob, and these husks, if intact, provide a good protection. Improved varieties do not always have such a full husk. On the other hand, kernels remaining inside an unhusked corn cob will, if they are not properly dried, quickly become mouldy, as the husk provides favourable conditions for mould growth.

The control of infestation is, to a large extent, dependent on good store management and making sure that material entering is not infested. The storeroom should always be kept as clean as possible. All material entering the store should be checked to see that it is not infested, and put into containers only after all the old product, dust, straw, etc. have been removed.

Airtight storage

Advantages
Sealed airtight storage provides a cheap method of insect control. Due to the respiration of the stored product and of any insects present, oxygen is used and carbon dioxide is formed, which results in the death of the insects. In order to accelerate this process, a lit candle can be placed in a tin at the top of the silo just before closing it. The burning candle quickly uses a great deal of the oxygen present. It is important to fill the silo to the top, as the oxygen present is then used up faster. Airtight storage will prevent further insects entering. Another advantage of airtight storage is the fact that moist outside air cannot enter the silo.

Disadvantages
An important disadvantage of airtight storage is that further drying of the produce in the store is impossible. Therefore, the crop needs to be well dried before placing it in the store.

Additionally, airtight storage is not convenient if the user regularly needs to open the stock to remove food. Clearly, when this happens, the whole principle of airtight storage is lost, because every time the store is opened fresh air enters. It is also extremely difficult to provide regular inspection of the product without letting air inside.

Control of pests in stores

As previously mentioned, a wide range of natural products find use in traditional storage systems, but nowadays these are tending to be replaced by commercial pesticides and poisons. Great care should be taken over the selection and use of such chemicals and advice should be sought.

Rodent poisons should be placed in containes and never allowed to come into contact with the food. The poisons should be changed regularly to avoid the pests developing resistance.

It should be remembered that rodents, after eating some types of poison, will often hide away and die. Other poisons make the animals very thirsty and so they leave the store in search of water.

In view of the dangers associated with rodent poisons, if their use is not properly controlled, consideration should be given to simpler traditional measures such as the use of cats, though their effectiveness is a matter of some debate.

In larger stores, electric 'insecto-cuters' are often used to control flying insects such as moths. Small comparatively cheap models are available.

The use of chemicals or traditional methods, while important, is no replacement for good store management and regular inspection. General cleanliness and care in handling containers is essential and any damage that occurs must be rectified immediately.

Storage characteristics of selected food commodities

Cereals and pulses

Dry cereals and pulses can be stored below their safe moisture level for periods of a year or more, under a wide range of temperatures, provided that, during storage, the moisture level does not rise and precautions against insects and pests are taken.

Seeds for sowing

The main aim in strong seed material is the preservation of its viability, or capacity to germinate. High temperatures can adversely affect seed viability so cool storage is necessary. An approximate 5°C decrease in the storage temperature will double the possible storage time. Moisture levels need to be low and, in general, every 1 per cent decrease in moisture content below 14 per cent will double the possible storage time.

Correct harvesting of seed material is vital. Seed that is harvested when not fully ripe will lose its viability sooner than mature seed.

Care must be taken in drying seed material. Because high temperatures can cause the embryos of the grains to break, maximum drying temperatures of 35°C are generally recommended. However, cereals can withstand temperatures of 40–45°C. In order to avoid overheating seed materials, full sun drying is not recommended.

Oil-bearing materials

Products containing oil, such as groundnuts, soya bean, sesame and coconut, are used either for direct consumption or for the extraction of oil. Oils contain free fatty acids and it is these which can develop odour and flavour changes called rancidity. High temperatures and exposure to light accelerate the development of rancidity. Some oilseeds, such as shea and coconut, are particularly susceptible to rancidity and therefore cannot be stored for long periods before use. Others, such as sunflower seeds, have fats that are far more resistant to rancidity development, and long-term storage is possible. The development of rancidity is also related to moisture content so safe moisture levels are important in oilseed crops.

Fungal growth is a particularly serious problem in certain oil-bearing materials as toxic aflatoxins may be produced.

Groundnuts, for example, are particularly susceptible, and the control of fungal growth is therefore extremely important. Such fungal growth can take place at moisture contents above 7 or 8 per cent, the actual level depending on the crop in question.

Root and tuber crops

These crops are very different to those previously discussed because of their high moisture content, normally 60–80 per cent when fresh. Two main effects have to be avoided: rotting and drying out.

Rotting is caused by storage under excessive humidity. Roots and tubers continue to respire during storage and this respiration increases with temperature. Due to this, better ventilation is necessary than with products such as dried grains.

During storage, a number of chemical changes occur in products of this type which may affect their firmness and flavour.

Root crops and tubers are, like all natural products, subject to attack by insects. They are particularly attractive to rats and mice, and rodent damage needs to be minimized during storage.

Roots and tubers have a natural dormancy period after which they start to sprout. The dormancy period varies with the crop and variety as well as with the storage temperature. Yams, for example, can be stored for about four months at normal temperatures between 25–35°C without sprouting. Potatoes, on the other hand, will start sprouting after five weeks at 15°C.

Often roots and tubers undergo a special treatment called 'curing' to increase their stability for storage. In this process the produce is stored under warm conditions, 25–35°C and high humidity, for a day or two. During this time a layer of special cells a few layers thick, known as 'cork cells', forms around the outer surface of the tuber. This cork layer greatly reduces the rate of drying out and also helps prevent infection by bacteria and fungi. During curing, the produce should be protected from full sunlight with, for example, large leaves, in order to maintain a high humidity around the produce. Curing has been widely used for improving the storage life of potatoes, yams and sweet potatoes but, until now, not for cassava. Cassava is more frequently waxed to improve its storage life.

Chill rooms provide an ideal method for the storage of root and tuber crops on a large scale. Systems that do not involve chill rooms are also widely used; usually thick-walled storage rooms with either natural or forced ventilation. It should be noted that the store should be ventilated during the coolest part of the day, i.e. at night, and isolated during the hottest time, thus trapping in the cool air.

Many roots and tubers can be stored by leaving them in the ground without harvesting. This has the following drawbacks:

- The land is occupied and not available for further cultivation.
- The product is not harvested at the optimum time.
- The crop is not protected from attack from termites, rats and thieves.

Fish

Fish is an extremely perishable food. Spoilage commences immediately after it is caught. This can make the fish unsuitable for consumption. The most important type of spoilage in fresh fish is bacterial deterioration. After the fish are caught, bacteria present on the surface and in the guts of the fish begin to multiply rapidly and invade the flesh. Bacterial slimes build up on the skin and in the gills, and the flesh is gradually broken down and gives off unpleasant fishy odours. Gutting and cleaning immediately after the fish is caught are important ways of reducing spoilage.

The rate of this bacterial spoilage is temperature dependent. Fish kept in melting ice (0°C) can remain edible for 15–30 days depending upon the species, whereas those kept at 5°C remain edible for 7–14 days and those at 20°C for only one day. In tropical countries therefore, fresh fish must be consumed as soon as possible after capture, if ice is not readily available or if it is too expensive. This results in limited distribution and problems in dealing with large catches during glut periods.

Fresh fish storage can be greatly assisted by the use of small refrigerators and chest freezers which are becoming increasingly common in many developing countries. These can offer a viable solution to small producers.

A variety of preservation methods such as drying, salting and smoking have been developed to prolong the shelf-life of the fish. Good storage is very important for dried, smoked and salted fish, which is particularly liable to attack by beetles. Large losses occur worldwide.

Meat

Meat, like fish, provides an ideal environment for the growth of micro-organisms. The shelf-life can be prolonged by chilling, freezing, salting, drying and smoking and, as with fish, the use of small chest freezers may be appropriate.

Fruit and vegetables

Most fruits and vegetables are eaten fresh due to their perishable nature. However, short-term price fluctuations occur: prices are higher at week-ends, holidays, and festivals. If farmers can store their produce, they can receive a better return for their crop.

Fruits and vegetables keep better when cooled but are damaged by freezing. They shrivel and wilt in air that is too dry. Different fruits and vegetables have different susceptibilities to temperature and humidity. For example, green leafy vegetables are very susceptible to spoilage, tomatoes are more resistant and certain commodities such as onions, carrots and oranges can be stored for much longer.

The control of temperature and humidity in the store is essential. Simple evaporative air-cooled cabinets can be constructed and these allow small farmers to store fruits and vegetables. In some areas, underground storage in pits and cellars is used, taking advantage of the naturally low temperatures underground. Hard vegetables like cabbages and carrots can be kept in this way.

Surface waxing and wrapping in paper can help to prolong the storage of certain fruits such as apples, pears and squashes. Such measures greatly reduce the spread of rot and decay from one fruit to another if any are damaged or bruised.

The essential point is that high quality produce will only come out from the store if high quality raw material is put in and if good in-store management is provided. Therefore, the selection of first quality produce and rejection of bruised and damaged produce is the first and most important step.

3
Traditional storage methods

Earthenware pots and gourds

IN THE TROPICS, earthenware pots and gourds (the hard dried outside skins of certain fruits and vegetables) are widely used for storing small quantities of foodstuffs. They need to be kept sheltered: above the kitchen where there are few insects is a good place. Such containers should be raised off the ground or put on plastic sheets to stop them absorbing moisture from below.

The storage characteristics of earthenware pots and gourds can be improved by treating them with varnish, paint, or oil, and by using sealed lids. Such lids can be sealed down with clay, oil, or with a piece of clean cloth dipped into wax which is then tied over the opening.

The contents should be regularly inspected to check for mould growth and infestation. If moisture has been absorbed then the food stuff should be removed and re-dried.

Suitable for: small quantities of cereals, beans, groundnuts, dried fruit and vegetables and seed material

Storage time: up to one year

Capacity: 5–30 litres

Cost: very low

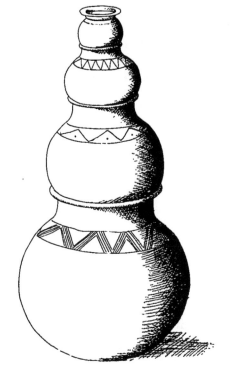

Earthen pots

Leaves

Traditional containers can be made out of leaves. They are made from a number of leaves or banana stems. Some are woven together or bound with string of sisal or other plant material. The leaves and the string are soaked in water to soften them before use and placed in a container such as a pot or basket which acts as a mould.

Dried vegetables are commonly stored in these containers. They are hung from the roof or on the veranda to complete their drying and finally are transferred to the kitchen of the main house. Production of leaf containers of this type requires considerable skill and people usually buy them from artisan producers.

Suitable for: dried fruits, vegetables and treacle

Storage time: up to one year if unopened

Capacity: variable

Materials: banana leaves, etc.

Cost: low

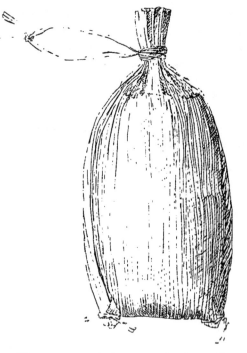

Storage container made from leaves used in Sri Lanka to store treacle

Bark

Bark is used to make storage containers. In East Africa sewn bark cylinders are used for this purpose. These traditional containers can have a capacity of 100kg of grain and are said to be fairly effective in preventing the entry of rats but offer little or no protection against insects. The skills required to make these bark containers are considerable.

Suitable for: cereals, particularly paddy and shelled maize

Storage time: up to three months

Capacity: 100kg

Cost: labour

Baskets

Baskets are widely used throughout the tropics for food storage. For certain products, good ventilation is required, so the baskets should not be placed too close together and if possible they should be raised off the ground. Woven baskets do not give much protection against insects. Baskets can be covered in plaster, mud or clay on both the inside and outside. This will improve protection against insects but reduce ventilation. Covered baskets are suitable for products that do not require ventilation. There is always a danger, however, of this covering cracking and then harbouring insects. Some improvement can be achieved by using a plastic sheet lining inside the basket.

Food stored in baskets should be well protected from rain, preferably in a dry area of the house or building.

Suitable for: cereals, pulses, oilseeds, potatoes, etc.

Storage time: up to nine months

Capacity: variable

Materials: reeds, grasses, palm leaves, bamboo, etc.

Cost: low, although considerable labour may be involved

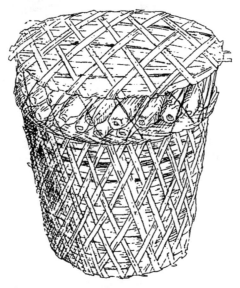

Baskets are widely used for food storage

Sacks

In general, jute sacks are cheaper than sacks made of cotton or sisal and are especially suitable for use in the dry tropics. Sacks give little protection against insects, rodents and moisture and are easily damaged during transport and handling.

To avoid moisture uptake they should not be placed on the ground but on plastic sheeting, waterproof canvas or, best of all, on wooden pallets. The last method allows good air circulation all around the sacks. Sacks should not be stacked against walls. Spaces should be left between the sacks to allow free air movement and paths left between stacks to allow inspection, cleaning and insect and rodent control.

It is important to clean used sacks thoroughly and to avoid cross-contamination. New sacks should be stored separately from old. The first step in sack cleaning is to shake out all debris vigorously. If the sacks are made of material that can be placed in hot water it is best to boil them or dip them and then dry them in the sun. Sacks that cannot be placed in water should be brushed and placed in the sun. They may be fumigated in closed containers to destroy insects.

Suitable for: cereals, pulses and dried fruit

Storage time: up to one year

Capacity: up to 60kg

Materials: jute, sisal and cotton

Cost: low

Sacks being used for storage should be stacked in a way that allows air to circulate

Basket silos

A range of different basket silos exists, but essentially a basket silo is cylindrical and is made of woven sheets of plant material such as elephant grass or reeds. Small silos may have a capacity of 100kg of grain with larger ones able to hold over half a tonne. Basket silos may be plastered with mud for extra protection. If they are not plastered on the inside, they are sometimes lined with straw or hessian. Such silos are reasonably durable and may be re-used from one season to the next.

Suitable for: cereals and pulses

Storage time: up to one year

Capacity: up to a tonne

Materials: elephant grass, reeds, sorghum stalks

Cost: local material, time spent on construction

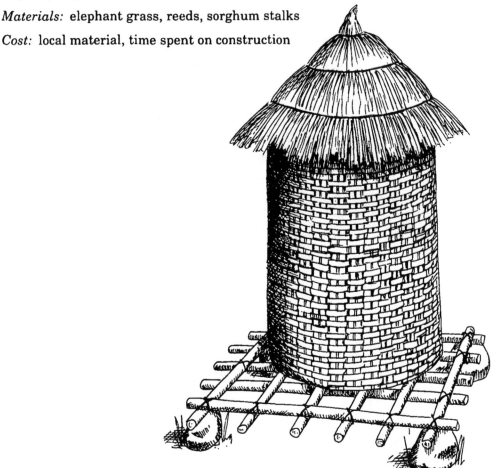

Basket silo on elevated platform for improved air circulation

Roof storage

Many foods, particularly cereals, are stored indoors in the roof of the house above the kitchen hearth. Sometimes special platforms are constructed. Heat and smoke from the fire helps to keep the product dry and to deter insects. One disadvantage is that it is difficult to protect the foodstuffs from rodents. Nevertheless the technique has considerable advantages in terms of low cost, control of insects and maintaining the cereals in a good dry condition.

Suitable for: cereals

Storage time: up to one year

Capacity: variable

Materials: may require wood for platform

Cost: wood for platform and labour

Roof storage

Maize cribs

Traditional maize cribs are suitable for the storage of maize cobs in semi-humid and dry tropics. The shape of the crib allows drying to proceed during storage using natural ventilation, provided that relative humidities are below 70 per cent. Cribs are preferably sited with their long side to the prevailing wind direction. Because of the narrow shape, usually 60–90cm in width, the drying process is better than in some traditional round cribs. Little protection is provided against insects. Traditional maize varieties with husks that cover the whole cob are protected reasonably well for three to six months. Removal of husks speeds up the grain drying and after reaching a safe moisture level, the maize is often shelled and stored in a less bulky way.

Suitable for: maize

Storage time: up to six months

Capacity: variable

Materials: variable

Cost: labour and materials

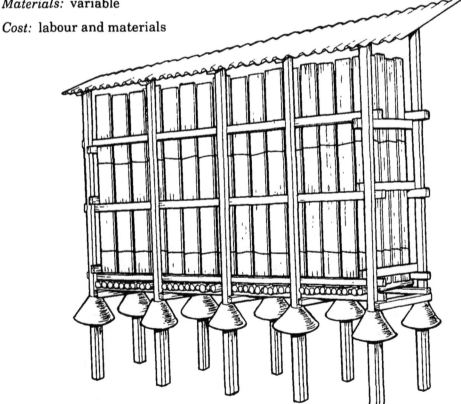

Maize crib

Underground pits

Storage in underground pits is a widely practised method in many tropical areas. Pits are cheap to construct, provided there is a sufficient depth of workable soil. They are of particular use in dry areas where wood for normal store construction may be in short supply. Traditional pits provide some protection from both insect and rodent attack, although termites can pose a problem. Mould damage often occurs in the vicinity of the pit sides and on the surface, due to migration of moisture from the soil and atmosphere. Good pit storage practice therefore depends on restricting the supply of air and moisture moving into the pit from the surrounding soil or from the atmosphere.

Traditional pit lining is carried out with plant materials (such as grass, straw and chaff or maize stalks), clay, cow dung or termite-mound soil. If only plant material is used, it probably does little more than keep the grain from direct contact with the soil around. The use of clay reduces water entry but does not prevent it totally.

After filling, the pits are closed and sealed with plant material and soil and they are usually plastered over. They may be cylindrical, rectangular or narrow-necked. They can be situated in raised ground, under dwellings or on puddled clay.

Suitable for: cereals, pulses and root crops

Storage time: up to one year

Capacity: variable

Materials: grass, straw, chaff and clay

Cost: labour

Clamp storage

Root crops and tubers are often cured and stored in field clamps. The typical design consists of a circular bed of straw or dried grass approximately 1.5m in diameter and 15cm thick, placed on well-drained ground. The freshly harvested tubers are heaped in a conical pile weighing 300–500kg on this straw bed and the whole pile is then covered with a similar pile of straw. The entire clamp is then covered with soil to a thickness of some 15cm. Soil is then removed from round the circumference of the clamp to give a drainage ditch. During cool moist periods, this basic clamp design is satisfactory.

In order to minimize the effects of direct sunshine or heavy rains, clamps may be protected by a thatched roof or positioned under trees. In hot dry areas it is necessary to ensure that the internal clamp temperature does not exceed 40°C since tubers will begin to deteriorate rapidly above this temperature. Clamps are modified to suit such conditions by applying a thicker soil cover and providing central and bottom ventilation holes to encourage air flow and the outflow of heat. Such ventilators are constructed from locally available materials such as straw, bamboo, drainpipes or timber. Frequent light rainfall can be advantageous since moistening of the soil lowers internal temperatures. Gentle wetting of the soil during hot dry periods should be considered.

If more than 500kg of tubers are to be stored at any one time, it is advisable to use several clamps or one single elongated structure, since internal temperatures are more difficult to control in very large clamps. In addition several smaller clamps reduce the possibility of loss of the whole stock by rotting.

Before making any specific recommendations for clamp storage, simple trials using locally available materials should be undertaken in order to determine the best design and location of clamps. Clamp storage of cassava by inter-layering with cassava leaves, and replacing the straw cover, first with cassava leaves and then with coconut fronds, appears to give better results.

Suitable for: tubers

Storage time: up to six months

Capacity: up to 500kg

Materials: grass, straw

Cost: labour

Small storehouses

A whole variety of small grain and food storehouses exists. The roof is generally constructed from thatch and the sides made from closely arranged sorghum stalks, reeds or bamboo. Air circulation under the floor and around the sides of stores provide better conditions than those found in roof stores. The store is generally cleaned thoroughly before filling with fresh grain and the old thatch is replaced. This reduces any rat or insect population left from the previous season. Good stacking is claimed to reduce insect attack. Stores can be more easily protected against rats than roof stores by fitting them with rat guards or baffles.

Suitable for: cereals and pulses

Storage time: up to one year

Capacity: variable

Materials: variable

Cost: labour and materials

Earth silos

Earth (i.e. mud and straw) storage structures are often used in dry tropical areas. They are less suitable for wet regions because water may readily enter via the walls. Earth silos may be made more waterproof by:

- using a mixture of 90 per cent loam or clay and 10 per cent cement for the construction of the walls;
- painting or coating the outer walls with coal tar, asphalt, oils or water-repellent paints;
- applying a layer of waterproof mortar to the walls.

Whitewashing will help to keep the silo cooler and it will fill in tiny cracks and openings. The product to be stored should be fully dried before placing it in the silo as further drying is difficult if not impossible.

Earth silos give better protection against insects than, for example, maize cribs. The silos should be protected from rain, which can cause severe damage. Earth silos are considerably cheaper to build than stone or concrete silos, and depend mainly upon local raw materials. Skilled labour is not needed. They do have the disadvantage of some moisture uptake and a comparatively short life.

Suitable for: pulses and cereals

Storage time: up to one year

Capacity: variable

Materials: earth, straw

Cost: labour

Earth silo

4
Improved storage techniques

Plastic bags

PLASTIC BAGS are widely used for storage in the humid and dry tropics. The product has to be dried well because, during storage, further drying is impossible as there is no air circulation. When plastic bags are closed well, airtight storage results, with all its advantages and disadvantages (see Chapter 2).

Plastic bags do not offer much protection against rodents, and they can be pierced by sharp seeds during transport and penetrated by insects. This can be reduced by putting a bag of tightly woven cotton inside the plastic bag. Plastic becomes weak or brittle after continued exposure to the sun and therefore no plastic package will last indefinitely. An advantage of transparent plastic is that the product remains visible which makes control more simple. Although the product may look good from the outside, however, it may have become musty within. Fertilizer bags cannot be used unless they have been very thoroughly cleaned.

Suitable for: sowing seed, cereals, pulses, groundnuts, copra

Storage time: six to nine months

Capacity: up to 60kg

Cost: fairly high

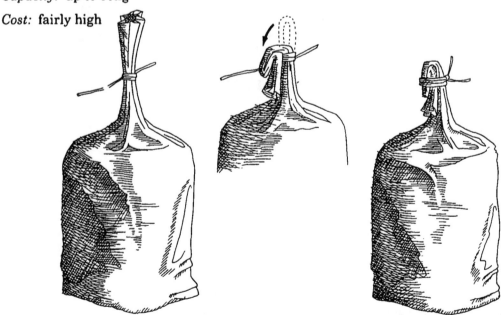

Closing a plastic bag to make it airtight

45-gallon metal drums

Small drums and water tanks are often available and can be used for storing crops, provided they have been well cleaned. When being used for storage, they should not be placed in full sunlight, but protected, preferably under a good roof, and insulated with a layer of straw to prevent large temperature changes. A tightly closed drum prevents the entry of insects. Grain should be well dried before filling.

Suitable for: cereals, pulses and seeds

Storage time: up to one year

Capacity: 50–200 litres

Materials: oil drums and water tanks

Cost: low, depending on availability

Metal drums

The Pusa bin

The Indian Pusa bin is essentially a square double-walled silo. Both the floor and the roof structure are also double-walled. The space between the two walls contains a layer of plastic sheeting to minimize the passage of water into the store. Provided the filling and emptying openings are well closed the store is extremely well sealed. In general, the walls are made from mud blocks but they can be made using a mixture of mud mixed with a small amount (10 per cent) of cement or made from fired bricks or concrete blocks. Grain should be well dried before storage.

Suitable for: cereals and pulses

Storage times: six to 12 months when storing well-dried crops

Capacity: 400kg to 3 tonnes depending on size

Materials: mud, cement or concrete, wood, plastic

Cost: medium/high; considerable skill required

Metal silos

A whole range of small metal silo designs exists, with silo capacities up to about 5 tonnes. The illustration shows a metal silo of 3-tonne capacity made of sheet metal 1mm thick welded at the seams. Some skill in welding is required to make the structure airtight. Silos can be made with overlapping sheets, bolted or riveted together.

The silo has two openings, one for filling at the top and one for emptying at the bottom. As in the case of metal drums, metal silos should not be placed in full sunlight, but sheltered to prevent dramatic temperature changes.

Some small silo designs incorporate a ventilation system operated by natural airflow. A rotating fan-like structure is placed on top of the silo and, when the flaps are open, the grain is ventilated by fresh cool air. Metal silos tend to be expensive.

Suitable for: cereals and pulses

Storage time: approximately one year

Capacity: up to 5 tonnes

Materials: sheet metal

Cost: medium/high

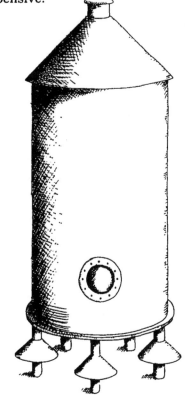

Metal silo of 3-tonne capacity

Brick and ferro-cement silos

Silos of this type are suitable for use in dry and wet tropical areas, but they should be protected from rain by a roof, and the base should be made from reinforced concrete or fired bricks. These silos are comparatively airtight and watertight, particularly when painted with rubber-based paints, coal tar or bitumen. A whole range of sizes and styles are possible. Three common types are brick, cement-stave and Thai ferro-cement silos.

The brick silo

As the name implies, this silo is made from bricks, placed on a reinforced foundation and covered by a concrete plate, with a manhole for filling and emptying. Brick silos are relatively easy to build and can store several tonnes of grain.

Suitable for: cereals and pulses

Storage time: up to one year

Capacity: up to 5 tonnes

Materials: bricks, cement, reinforcing rod, wood for moulds, sheet metal

Cost: medium/high

The cement-stave silo

The cement-stave silo is more durable than the brick silo but also somewhat more expensive. It does cost less, however, than a metal silo of the same size. Cement-stave silos are often raised off the ground on pillars or placed on brick foundations. The walls are made from cement slabs held together with strong iron wire and the covering slab is made of concrete.

Suitable for: cereals and pulses

Storage time: up to one year

Capacity: up to 10 tonnes

Materials: cement, sand, iron and wire

Cost: medium/high

The Thai ferro-cement silo

Ferro-cement is made of wire mesh (for example chicken-wire), sand and cement and it is strong and durable. Ferro-cement silos can be made in almost any shape. The Thai ferro-cement silo has a conical shape and is waterproof and airtight. The base is saucer-shaped and is made of two layers of reinforced concrete with a layer of bitumen, asphalt paper, plastic or metal foil in between. The frame of the walls is made from water pipes or bamboo poles and reinforcing rods, which support an inside and outside layer of wire mesh. The mesh structure is filled and smeared with mortar of a paste-like consistency: 1 part of standard cement, 1.75 parts sand with the optional addition of a plasticizer to improve workability.

Suitable for: cereals and pulses

Storage time: nine to 12 months

Capacity: 4–6 tonnes, depending on the size

Materials: cement, sand, aggregate, mortar plasticizer, sealant for base, paint, chicken-wire, no. 2 rod, water pipe. When using bamboo poles instead of water pipes, the walls have to be much thicker, requiring more cement.

Cost: medium/high

Storage in ventilated huts

The aims of this type of storage are to offer protection against rodents, sun, rain and groundwater and, by providing ventilation, to prevent fungus growth and rotting. As this method offers hardly any protection against insects, it is less suitable for long-term storage of cereals and pulses. This storage method is very suitable for the storage of root crops.

For construction, locally available materials should be used: bamboo, planks, woven mats in a wooden frame, etc. For protection against rats and termites, the huts can be built on poles, at least 75cm in height, with rat baffles fixed on them. If the walls are made of planks they should overlap like roof tiles with some space between them so that sunlight cannot enter but ventilation is still possible. The roof of wood or thatch should be overhanging for protection against sun and rain. Inside the hut, the products should be piled in boxes or on shelves or racks along the wall, in such a way that air can move freely between them. Regular inspection of stored products is necessary.

Suitable for: cereals, pulses, root crops

Storage time: variable

Capacity: variable

Materials: local building materials

Cost: medium/high

Improved pit storage

Roofing

The roofing of a pit can be made of metal sheet, sealed with mud/dung or bitumen, or polythene sheet. A temporary shelter over the pit site gives protection from rain but should be removed in the dry season to ensure drying by evaporation, because a shelter does not prevent lateral movement of water into the pit.

Improving pit linings

- Coating the walls of the pit with mud/dung/straw mixture: the grain remains much drier than in unimproved pits.
- The product is put into well-sealed plastic bags, which are placed in the pit: this allows part of the product to be removed without letting air and moisture into the rest of it.

- Platic lining: the pit is lined with a plastic sheet or cut-open plastic bags which are sealed together. The disadvantage is that the plastic lining can be damaged easily.
- Ferro-cement lining: a pit can be made airtight and watertight by using ferro-cement to line the pit: two layers of mortar (cement:sand 1:3 with as little water as possible to make a paste), 2.5–3cm thick, with a chicken-wire reinforcement between the layers.

A water barrier can be achieved by incorporating a bitumen layer between the two mortar layers or by applying a cement/bitumen emulsion layer as a final lining.

Suitable for: cereals, pulses and root crops

Storage time: up to one year

Capacity: variable

Materials: metal sheet, mud/dung/straw or plastic or ferro-cement lining

Cost: medium

5
Socio-economic context

IN AFRICA, ASIA, and South/Central America, it is usually women who produce and process food, either for household consumption or for sale. Food security is a particularly important priority for women, since they are often the last to eat in a household at times of famine. In times of plenty, selling food generates income for women who generally have less access to cash than men do. For both these reasons, it is valuable to be able to store food after harvest so as not to be compelled to sell it at low prices. Appropriate storing techniques can prolong the life of foodstuffs, and/or protect the quality, thereby keeping it for lean times of the year.

The value of securing food availability for longer periods has to be judged by food processors against the cost of improving storage techniques. If the food is for household consumption, women are unlikely to make a large cash outlay, but it might be possible for those running a small business, as long as the initial investment can be paid back. Existing local methods are usually low-cost, so adapting what is already there, rather than introducing new technology, is often a more realistic economic option for households.

Appraisal

Storage is not a new idea for farmers, since they have been developing ways of storing produce for hundreds of years. Given the materials and resources available, traditional methods may be the most effective.

Some farmers, on the other hand, may decide to take advantage of greater choice, by adopting new modifications or technology. Before initiating technology development work with women food processors, it is important to assess the need for improvements. This can only be done by the producers themselves. They are the only people who know enough about their own particular priorities, constraints and circumstances to make decisions about their choice of technology. Furthermore, the whole process of technology development should be in their hands since only they can shape and control their own plans to their own satisfaction.

Here are some ideas for the kind of questions that can be usefully discussed with producers during a preliminary appraisal.

Needs and opportunities assessment checklist
- Are there problems with existing storage techniques? If yes, what kind of problems: rodents, insects, deterioration, other?
- Do the producers find that the disadvantages of existing storage techniques are greater than the advantages?
- Would improved storage reduce the loss of produce?
- Would better storage increase the quality of produce for sale or consumption?
- Would the producers be in a position to keep surplus produce stored away, rather than having to sell any extra produce immediately?

- Would the producers be in a position to sell any extra produce? For example, would they have enough time, labour and access to both transport and marketing channels?
- Would the improvements in storage increase the profit earned by the producers?
- Would the producers have time for learning about improved techniques for collecting materials, and for making the new equipment needed for storage?
- Would the producers have access to enough money to pay for the storage materials?
- Would resource-poor producers have access to the new technical knowledge and skills required for producing, maintaining and using the new technology?
- Weighing up the likely benefits against the resource constraints, is it worth making the investment of time, money and effort in improving the storage?
- Will women have control over the income they earn?

If the answer to the majority of the questions above is 'yes,' then a more detailed appraisal of possible technical improvements to the storage methods is probably appropriate.

Technology choice

When helping producers to choose, adapt or develop improved storage methods, the following should be considered.

Technical considerations

The efficiency of different methods
The efficiency of different storage methods can only be measured by trying them out in the field. For example, the amount of produce lost using a new method should be compared with the losses resulting from equivalent existing methods. The results from these tests, carried out by a small sample of producers, will be invaluable information for other producers when they are deciding whether it is worth investing in new technology. Producers should be encouraged to set targets which must be met by new technology. For example, they might demand that an average of at least 75 per cent of the produce survives using a particular storage method.

Availability of materials
The choice of technology depends partly on what materials are required (cement, plastic sheets, insecticides, wood, water, screening), and whether they are available locally.

Climate and ecology

The storage methods should be appropriate to the temperature, average rainfall, winds, and type of soil. Seasonal variations in climatic conditions should be taken into account where relevant.

Use of product

The choice made will be affected by whether the product needs to be readily accessible. If the food is to be eaten by the household, then produce should be within easy reach. If it is for sale, then it is often necessary to store it for longer periods. The length of time in storage will be affected by the time of harvests and markets.

Type of product

The kind of food to be stored must be taken into account. The different classes of produce – cereals, pulses, seeds, oil-bearing materials, roots and tuber crops, fish, meat, vegetables – will all have to be treated differently. For example, fresh fish undergoes bacterial deterioration as soon as it leaves the water and needs to be kept in melting ice, while pulses are likely to be spoiled by insects and need a protective container rather than a drop in temperature.

Quantity

The amount of product to be stored will influence the choice made since some technologies can store far greater quantities than others. For example, basket silos can hold up to half a tonne of cereal while a sack can only carry up to 60kg.

Economic considerations

Costs

Food processors will look at the costs of different methods when working out the viability of different options for improving their storage methods. If the produce is for consumption, rather than sale, then the new technology will not pay back the investment. On the other hand, if the amount of food for sale increases, then the investment can be paid back over time. The following calculation is useful for businesses to estimate this 'payback' period:

Existing profit
- Calculate the monthly costs of the business. This shold include both the fixed costs (e.g. rent, loan repayments, the amount put aside for buying or replacing equipment) and the variable costs which change according to the season or amount being produced (e.g. materials, labour and transport).
- Calculate the monthly total gross income of the business. This should include the total amount of cash received for all the goods sold. If the processor does not keep a record of money coming in, then an estimate can be made using the production level and multiplying it by the price.
- Subtract the costs from the gross income in order to get an estimate of the average monthly net income.

Potential profit with new technology
- Follow the same procedure outlined above, but this time adjust the cost of replacing equipment, materials and the value of sales (which will all probably be higher) according to the changes resulting from the adoption of new storage technology.
- With this information, decide whether the increase in income warrants the extra time, money and effort demanded by a particular new storage technology.

Income and credit of producers

Plainly, those with the lowest incomes can least afford to store food. A common constraint is that produce has to be sold off immediately to pay off debts to landowners or creditors. This is the most widespread reason for deciding that investing in new storage technology is impossible.

If a relatively large cash outlay is required for storage, households who consume their own produce may decide they cannot afford the new equipment, even once their debts are paid. For the more expensive storage methods, it will probably be only small businesswomen who would consider the investment worthwhile.

Access to credit is often dependent on where people live (banks and lending institutions may not reach into rural areas), educational levels (illiterate people find it harder to borrow money), and on being able to raise collateral. Adopting new storage methods may only be possible for low-income women if they are given assistance with literacy and numeracy, and possibly some kind of group training, in order to secure a loan.

Social and cultural considerations

Women's time

Women usually have a substantial burden of work. They are often responsible for most of the household work and, in many places, for agricultural or horticultural production as well. Paid employment, or running businesses are the main time commitments for other women. For this reason, many women will simply not have the time to spend on constructing extensive storage facilities. For others, where at least some of their work is seasonal, there may only be sufficient time for building better storage facilities during some months.

Once the equipment is constructed, women will have to consider how much time is required for placing the food in storage, and maintaining the facilities in good order. If this work can be interwoven or alternated with other tasks then the new methods may be more popular with women. For some, an additional time input will be perceived as worthwhile only if the increase in income is sufficient. Priorities and time commitments will vary considerably between individuals and with different places. The time viability of new methods must be judged by women themselves, since only they can take into account all the aspects of their particular workload and time constraints.

Skills/training

Women who have been involved in food processing will have knowledge and skills

in this area already. For instance, existing methods may include storing products in leaves sealed with clay, bark containers, in houses and underground pits. Nevertheless, processors may wish to develop their methods further in order to store and protect food for longer, but they do not always have the necessary knowledge and skills. Adopting new storage methods is likely to require some technical training. This will only be possible if the women are in a position to invest the time in learning and developing new skills.

In addition to technical training, for example, in making a new type of silo, women may need training or advice on maintenance, health and safety regulations, business management, marketing, group organization, literacy, numeracy, accounting, confidence building, and so on. In some instances, one set of skills are not useful unless combined with others. The need for skills will depend upon the circumstances of the individual or household; most importantly, on whether the food is for sale or for home consumption. The adoption of new storage technology will depend largely upon giving women processors the opportunity to assess their skill-development needs and by offering appropriate advice, assistance and training in response.

Ownership

The amount people are prepared to invest in new technology may depend partly upon who owns the equipment and facilities. In some places, women will only invest in new technology if they have total ownership of it, while in other places, storage may be collectively owned and so costs can be shared. The decisions concerning ownership will be affected by existing relationships, government policy, and the past history of co-operation between households, businesses and communities.

Cultural policies

Social, cultural or religious practices may play a part in decisions about which technology to use. In some places, men handle some produce while women deal with other kinds of produce, and the roles cannot be reversed.

The design of storage buildings may have a particular cultural significance, reflecting the status of the owner in a distinctive way. If this status is valued, the owner may prefer to modify the existing building rather than replace it with a new one.

If people are satisfied with one kind of material, practice, or method, it may be wise to build on it rather than supplant it with an alternative. For example, farmers who are used to building with mud bricks may wish to build their storage facilities out of a similar material.

Monitoring and evaluation

While the technology is being developed, it is important to monitor progress, in order to straighten out problems, build on developments, and record successes and failures. Monitoring and evaluation should be based on judgements made by the women processors.

It is also useful for staff in a project context to appraise their own efforts. Progress should be measured in areas of interest which may include: level of technical skills, innovative capacity, quality of produce, level of sales, level of income, access to credit, numbers of processors involved, and so on.

At the end of the development phase, when the new technology has been either adopted or rejected, it is important to evaluate what has happened. When evaluating, information collected during monitoring should be used to measure whether project objectives are being met. For instance, during and at the end of a project, producers may want to know whether the new storage has increased sales or provided more food for the family. As soon as success is recognized, steps can be taken to consolidate it, and once failure is spotted, the problems can be identified and dealt with. Evaluations can be used as evidence of good or bad innovation, from which others can learn, and for long-term planning. For example, if produce lasts longer with the improved storage, and more producers become interested in learning the new techniques, then other organizations may support further training work.

Impact should be measured in those areas of interest which were considered during monitoring. In addition, the investigation of socio-economic impact should be considered: who benefits and how is additional income or time distributed between and within households or businesses; who controls the income or time; what is the extra money or time spent on; who consumes any extra food which becomes available; what positive and negative effects does the new technology have on the individual women processor, her household, and her community.

6
Case studies

Improvements to traditional grain stores in Zambia

TRADITIONAL STORAGE BINS of varying sizes made of woven wood or bamboo and raised on a low platform are extensively and successfully used by farmers in Zambia to store maize and other grains such as sorghum. The grain, if properly dried, will keep reasonably well for up to 10 months.

However, in the late 1970s, with the introduction of new hybrid and composite maize, farmers faced a major problem with insects and rodents during storage. It was found that even though the new varieties of maize yielded considerably more than local varieties, they did not have the same resistance to infestation in the field and during storage. This resulted in approximately 50 per cent post-harvest loss of the new varieties of maize grain in storage and, at the end of the storage season, the grain was so damaged that it could only be used to feed chickens.

The Zambian Ministry of Agriculture responded by requesting the Mt Makulu Research Station (MRS) to try and solve the problems. MRS put forward and transferred improved storage techniques to farmers which involved:

- Drying the maize to 12 per cent moisture content
- Treating with 1 per cent malathion dust
- Storing the dry, treated maize in one of three types of improved solid-walled bins that had been developed by the MRS.

The improved traditional bin

The simplest and cheapest new bin design is 'the improved traditional bin.' In this, a woven basket made of sticks or split bamboo is covered with soil. The walls slope towards a covered manhole in the top, with an outlet near the bottom. The bin is placed on a wooden platform and covered by a thatched roof.

Advantages
- The maize keeps well: good protection is provided against insects and rodents.
- only metal rodent baffles and some nails need to be purchased.
- The villagers are familiar with the building techniques.

Disadvantages
- Maintenance is necessary every year and the whole construction will last less time than a Ferrumbu or a cement-plastered basket (see below).
- There might be problems with termites because of the use of soil.
- Difficult to make theft-proof.

The cement-plastered basket

The second, slightly more expensive store, 'the cement-plastered basket' is similar to the improved traditional bin, except that it is plastered with a cement mortar instead of soil and it is built on a foundation made of stones for increased durability.

Advantages
- The maize keeps well.
- Little maintenance is required (only repairs to the roof). Comparatively cheap.

- Useful life greater than the improved traditional bin.

Disadvantages
- The size is limited by how big the basket can be made. A tall bin will require a big roof.
- As the structure is made of organic materials, there can be a slight risk of termite attack, if the basket is not completely covered with mortar.

The Ferrumbu

The last model proposed is made of ferrocement and is called 'the Ferrumbu.' It looks similar to the cement-plastered basket, but the 'basket' is actually constructed from chicken-wire and cement. For field use a roof is recommended.

Advantages
- Provides good protection against insects, rodents, termites and thieves, and the maize keeps well.
- Long lasting with little maintenance.
- Range of sizes possible, with up to 115 bags capacity.

Disadvantages
- Somewhat expensive.
- Possible unavailability of cement and chicken wire in remote rural areas.
- Involves unfamiliar building technique.

These new technologies have helped to reduce grain loss in storage considerably, depending on the type of bin used. The improved traditional bin has had the widest acceptance, being cheap and easy to construct. The three systems provide farmers with a choice, depending on availability of materials, skills and amount of material to be stored. (G. Nygaard Pedersen, Mt Makulu Research Station, Ministry of Agriculture and Water Development, Zambia)

Flexible solar heat disinfestation devices for domestic and rural storage of cereals in the tropics

It is estimated that nearly 75 per cent of the grain produced in countries such as India does not receive adequate pest-control measures. This case study, from the Central Food Technology Research Institute in India, describes a new approach to control infestation of grain prior to storage.

If grain is heated to 60°C and held at that temperature for ten minutes, all stored product insects and their stages (larvae and eggs) are killed. The case study describes a simple method by which this can be done.

The grain is packed into large pouches made of standard black high density polythene. A typical one square metre area pouch will hold 25kg of wheat, sorghum or rice and is spread out so that the thickness of the layer is three to four centimetres. After closing the mouth of the pouches, they are covered with a sheet of clear polythene to give a greenhouse effect and laid out in the sun. Typically, in India, they reach a temperature above 60°C in four to six hours. The temperature can be checked by inserting a piece of straw that has been dipped in paraffin wax through the plastic into the grain mass. The wax melts at 60°C.

There has been great success using this system to treat quantities between 1kg and 100kg of various grains, oilseeds, pulses and ground flour; the exposure time depending on the commodity.

It seems likely that if the grain is tipped out of the pouch when hot into a thin layer, it would also lose moisture. This simple system would allow householders and small farmers to maintain their stored grain in good condition at comparatively low cost. (Krishnamurthy, T.S. *et al.*)

References

Action/Peace Corps/Vita manual (1977) *Small Farm Grain Storage.*

Adams, J.J. (1977) 'The Evaluation of Losses in Maize Stored on a Selection of Small Farms in Zambia, with Particular Reference to Methodology.' *Tropical Stored Products Information,* 33.

Agromisa (1982) *The Storage of Tropical Agricultural Products.* Agromisa, The Netherlands.

Anon (1978) 'Conserving Grain on the Small Farm in the Tropics.' *Tropical Science,* 20 (2).

Anon (not dated) *Handbook of Crop Storage and Marketing.* Ministry of Agriculture, Government of Botswana.

Anon (1981) *Tropical Stored Products Information,* 42.

Anon (not dated) 'Underground Storage of Crops: A Selected Bibliography.' *Tropical Stored Products Information,* 23.

Anon (1975) *Workshop on Food Preservation and Storage.* Tanzania.

Clarke, J.H. (not dated) 'Fungi in Stored Products.' *Tropical Stored Products Information,* 14.

Cole, D.B. (not dated) *Handbook of Crop Storage.* Regional Ministry of Agriculture and Natural Resources, Sudan.

Coursey, P. (not dated) 'The Storage Behaviour of Yams.' *Tropical Stored Products Information,* 7.

Coveney, R.D. (not dated) 'Sacks for the Storage of Food Grains.' *Tropical Stored Products Information,* 17.

FAO Publications (1970) *The Handling and Storage of Food.* Rome, Italy.

FAO Publications (1975) *Storage of Foodgrain: A guide for extension workers.* Rome Italy.

FAO Publications (not dated) *Food Preservation Series in Rural Home Techniques.* Rome, Italy.

GATE Publications (1978) *Manual on Improved Farm and Village-level Grain Storage Methods.* Eschborn, Germany.

GATE Publications (1978) *Improved Village and Farm Level Grain Storage Methods.* Eschborn, Germany.

Giles, P.H. (not dated) 'Maize Storage: The problem of today.' *Tropical Stored Products Information,* 14.

Golob, P. (not dated) 'Improvements in Maize Storage for the Smallholder Farmer.' *Tropical Stored Products Information,* 50. TDRI Storage Dept.

Golob, P., Ngulube, F., Nhango, V. and Kumwenda, W. (not dated) *The Effect of Store Diameter on the Rate of Drying of Maize Stored on the Cob in Malawi.* Crop Storage Project, Buumbwe Research Station, Malawi.

Greelye, Martin (not dated) *The Indian Grain Storage Project 1974–1978.* Institute of Development Studies.

Hindmarch, P.S. (1977) 'The Long-Term Storage of Hybrid Maize Seed in Zambia Using Polythene-lined Sacks.' *Tropical Science.*

Hoppe, T. (1986) *Tropical Science*, 26 (1).

Krall, S. (1984) 'A New Threat to Farm-level Maize Storage in West Africa.' *Tropical Stored Products Information*, 50.

Krishnamurthy, K. (not dated) 'Storage of Foodgrains in India.' *Tropical Stored Products Information*, 25.

Krishnamurthy, T.S., Muralidharan, N. and Muthu, M., *Infestation Control and Protection*, Central Food Technological Research Institute, India.

Lepigre, A.L., and Pointel, J.G. (1971) 'Protection of Maize Stored in Traditional Togolese Granaries.' *Tropical Stored Products Information*, 21.

Lipton, M., Cook, I. and Nair, N. *Cost-Benefit Analysis of Crop Storage Improvements: A South India Pilot Study.* Institute of Development Studies.

Pattinson, I. 'The History and Organization of Stored Products Work in the Gambia.' *Tropical Stored Products Information*, 9.

Patel, A.U., Adesuyi, S. A. (1975) 'Crib Storage of Maize under Tropical Village Conditions, in the Ibadan Area of Nigeria.' *Tropical Stored Products Information*, 29.

Pimentel, David (1978) *Of Millet, Mice and Men: Traditional and Invisible Technology Solutions to Post-harvest Losses in Mali.* World Food Pests Losses and the Environment; Westview Publications.

Report of a Pilot Project (1977) *Appropriate Technology for Grain Storage.* Community Development Trust Fund of Tanzania. ECA Pubs.

Stirling, H.G. (not dated) 'A Comparison of Storage Costs for Structures of Different Materials.' *Tropical Stored Products Information*, 22.

Taiwo-Williams, S.K. (not dated) 'Grain Storage in the Western State of Nigeria (case histories) Success or Failure.' *Tropical Stored Products Information*, 25.

Taylor, R.W.D. and Webley, D.J. (1979) 'Constraints on the Use of Pesticides to Protect Stored Grain in Rural Conditions.' *Tropical Stored Products Information*, 38.

World Food Programme FAO Pub. (1983) *Food Storage Manual.*

Contacts

The following can be contacted for further information on storage and experiences in planning storage projects. Some of these institutions have developed their own equipment which has been or is being used in the field.

Africa

CDTF
Community Development Trust Fund, P.O. Box 9421, Dar-es-Salaam, Tanzania.

IITA
International Institute of Tropical Agriculture, Oyo Road, PMB 5320, Ibadan, Oyo State, Nigeria.

WARDA
West African Rice Development Association, P.O. Box 1019, Monrovia, Liberia.

IRAT
Institut de Recherche – Agriculture Tropicale, Niaouli, Benin.

Ministry of Agriculture, Chilalo Agriculture Development Unit
Storage and Processing of Agriculture Product Unit, P.O. Box 3376, Addis Ababa, Ethiopia.

Asia

ICRISAT
International Crops Research Institute for Semi-Arid Tropics, Patancheru, P.O. Andhra Pradesh 502 324, India.

IRRI
International Rice Research Institute, P.O. Box 933, Manila 1099, The Philippines.

Europe

Agromisa
P.O. Box 41, 6700 AA, Wageningen, The Netherlands.

GATE
German Appropriate Technology Exchange, Postfach 5180, D-6236 Eschborn, Germany.

GRET
Groupe de Recherche et Echanges Technologiques, 213 rue Lafayette, Paris 75010, France.

IDS
Institute of Development Studies, University of Sussex, Brighton BN1 9RE, UK.

IT
Intermediate Technology, Myson House, Railway Terrace, Rugby CV21 3HT, UK.

KIT
Royal Tropical Institute, Mauritskade 63, 1092 A D, Amsterdam, The Netherlands.

NRI
Natural Resources Institute, Central Avenue, Chatham Maritime, Kent ME4 4TB, UK.

Silsoe College
Department of Storage, Silsoe, Bedfordshire MK45 4DT, UK.

Latin America

CIMMYT
Centro Internacional de Mejoramiento de Maiz y Trigo, Londres 40, Mexico 6, D.F. Mexico.

CIAT
Centro Internacional de Agricultura Tropical, Apartado Aereo 67–13, Cali, Colombia, South America.

Middle East

Ministry of Agriculture, Agricultural Research Organization
Institute for Technology and Storage of Agricultural Products, Division of Stored Products, Yafo, Israel.

North America

IDRC
International Development Research Centre, 60 Queen Street, Ottawa, Canada.

Cornell University, New York State Agricultural Experiment Station
Geneva, NY 14456, USA.

Brace Research Institute
Agricultural Engineering Building, McDonald College of McGill University, Ste Anne de Bellevue, Quebec H9X 3V9, Canada.

Board of Science and Technology for International Development
Commission on International Relations, National Research Council, 2101 Constitution Avenue, Washington DC 20418, USA.

www.ingramcontent.com/pod-product-compliance
Lightning Source LLC
Jackson TN
JSHW052134131224
75386JS00037B/1273